I0406828

# DANIEL GRAD

# Teaching Children to Start a Business

## Give Your Kids Financial Freedom

ISBN: 9798862080339
Imprint: Independently published

# Table of Contents

# Introduction

In today's rapidly evolving world, the concept of entrepreneurship is no longer reserved for adults in suits or tech-savvy millennials. The seeds of business acumen can, and perhaps should, be sown at a much younger age. Teaching children about business is not merely about instilling in them the desire to make money or start a venture, but it's about equipping them with a mindset that sees problems as opportunities, challenges as learning experiences, and failures as stepping stones to success.

The importance of nurturing an entrepreneurial spirit in children cannot be overstated. In an era where traditional job security is waning and the gig economy is on the rise, the ability to think creatively, innovate, and adapt is becoming increasingly vital. By introducing children to the world of business, we are not just preparing them for potential future careers as entrepreneurs; we are also teaching them valuable life skills. These skills, such as critical thinking, decision-making, and risk assessment, will serve them well in any path they choose to tread.

Furthermore, the journey of teaching children about business is not a one-size-fits-all approach. Each child is unique, with their own set of interests, strengths, and aspirations.

This book aims to provide a comprehensive guide that can be tailored to fit the individual needs and curiosities of each young learner. Through real-life examples, interactive exercises, and practical advice, we will explore the multifaceted world of business, from the initial spark of an idea to the intricacies of execution.

As we delve into the subsequent chapters, it's essential to remember that the goal is not necessarily to produce the next generation of CEOs or startup founders, though that would be a welcome outcome. Instead, our primary objective is to foster a mindset that is curious, resilient, and proactive. In doing so, we are setting our children up for success, whether they choose to enter the business world or any other sphere of life. So, let's embark on this exciting journey together, unlocking the vast potential that lies within our young ones and paving the way for a brighter, more entrepreneurial future.

## 1.1 The Importance of Entrepreneurship for Children

Entrepreneurship is not just about starting businesses and making money; it's a mindset that empowers individuals to take initiative, solve problems, and create value in society. When children are introduced to entrepreneurial thinking at a young age, they develop a unique set of skills and perspectives that can benefit them in various aspects of their lives.

Firstly, entrepreneurship nurtures creativity and innovation. As children explore the world of business, they are encouraged to think outside the box, come up with novel solutions, and view challenges as opportunities rather than obstacles. This creative problem-solving ability is invaluable, not just in the business realm but in everyday life situations as well.

Moreover, entrepreneurship teaches children about responsibility and accountability. When they embark on a venture, they quickly realize the importance of making decisions and bearing the consequences of their actions. This sense of ownership and responsibility can translate to better decision-making in personal life, academics, and future professional endeavors.

Additionally, entrepreneurship provides a practical understanding of financial literacy.

In a world where financial knowledge is paramount, children who grasp the basics of budgeting, saving, and investing from a young age are better equipped to make informed financial decisions as adults. They learn the value of money, the significance of hard work, and the importance of financial planning.

Furthermore, the journey of entrepreneurship instills resilience and perseverance in children. Every entrepreneur, regardless of age, faces setbacks and failures.

However, these challenges teach children to bounce back, adapt, and persist in the face of adversity. Such resilience is a life skill that aids them in navigating the ups and downs of life with grace and determination.
Lastly, entrepreneurship fosters a sense of independence and self-confidence. As children take their ideas from conception to reality, they gain a profound sense of accomplishment. This boosts their self-esteem and reinforces the belief that they have the power to shape their destinies.

Introducing children to entrepreneurship is not just about grooming the next generation of business leaders; it's about equipping them with a holistic set of skills and values that will serve them well in all walks of life. Whether they choose to become entrepreneurs or not, the lessons they learn from the entrepreneurial journey are bound to enrich their lives in countless ways.

## 1.2 How This Book Can Help

Creativity and innovation are paramount - it's essential to equip our children with the skills and mindset that will serve them throughout their lives. This book is designed as a comprehensive guide to introduce the foundational concepts of entrepreneurship to young minds.

By delving into the intricacies of starting a business, from the initial spark of an idea to the practicalities of operations, we aim to demystify the entrepreneurial journey for children. We believe that by understanding the basics of business, children can develop a proactive mindset, learn the value of hard work and dedication, and appreciate the importance of resilience in the face of challenges.

Moreover, this guide serves as a bridge between theoretical knowledge and real-world application, ensuring that young readers can not only grasp the concepts but also see how they play out in real-life scenarios.

Through relatable examples, engaging narratives, and actionable advice, this book endeavors to inspire a new generation of young entrepreneurs, fostering a sense of confidence and enthusiasm for creating, innovating, and making a positive impact in their communities and beyond. In essence, this book is more than just a manual on business; it's a tool for nurturing the leaders, problem-solvers, and visionaries of tomorrow.

# Chapter: Understanding the Basics of Business

Understanding the basics of business is akin to laying the foundation for a towering skyscraper. At its core, a business is an organized entity that seeks to provide goods or services to consumers in exchange for monetary compensation. This simple exchange is the heartbeat of economies worldwide, driving innovation, employment, and societal progress.

However, the simplicity of this exchange belies the complexity beneath. Every business operates within a market, a dynamic environment where supply meets demand. The dance between these two forces determines the price of goods and services, and by extension, the profitability of businesses. A keen understanding of market dynamics is essential for any entrepreneur or business professional. Recognizing where there's an unmet demand or where supply is waning can be the difference between a thriving enterprise and a failing one.

Yet, beyond market dynamics, the essence of business also lies in its financial underpinnings. Profit and loss are the measures of a business's success and sustainability. Profit isn't just about money; it's a reflection of value creation. When a business earns a profit, it signifies that it has provided a service or product that holds more value to the consumer than the cost of its production.

Conversely, a loss indicates a discrepancy between the perceived value and the production cost, signaling a need for adjustment and adaptation.

Furthermore, while the tangible aspects of business, such as products, services, and finances, are crucial, the intangible elements often hold equal weight. The culture of a business, its mission, values, and its approach to ethical considerations, shapes its public perception and internal operations. A business with a strong, positive culture is more likely to attract loyal customers and dedicated employees, both of which are invaluable assets in the competitive world of commerce.

Understanding the basics of business is a journey into the heart of human exchange, value creation, and societal progression. It's about recognizing opportunities, navigating challenges, and constantly evolving in response to the ever-changing dance of supply and demand. As we delve deeper into the world of business, we come to appreciate its multifaceted nature, where strategy, finance, ethics, and innovation intertwine to create the vibrant tapestry of modern commerce.

## 2.1 What is a Business?

At its most foundational level, a business is an intricate tapestry of ideas, efforts, and transactions that collectively aim to offer something of value to a specific audience or market. This value proposition, whether it's a tangible product or an intangible service, is designed to fulfill a particular need or desire, and in return, the business seeks compensation, typically in the form of monetary profit. But to understand a business fully, one must delve deeper into its multifaceted nature.

A business is not just a static entity; it's a living, breathing organism that evolves over time. It starts as a seed—an idea. This idea, once nurtured with the right resources, planning, and dedication, can grow into an establishment that impacts not just the owner or the employees but the broader community and, in some cases, the world at large. From the local bakery that provides fresh bread to the neighborhood to tech giants that revolutionize how we communicate globally, businesses shape our daily experiences and societal structures.

Furthermore, businesses are also a reflection of human ambition and creativity. Entrepreneurs, the individuals who venture into starting businesses, often do so driven by a vision. This vision could be solving a persistent problem, introducing an innovative solution, or simply expressing one's passion.

The journey of entrepreneurship is filled with challenges and uncertainties, but it's this very journey that often leads to societal advancements and progress.

In the broader economic landscape, businesses play a pivotal role. They are engines of job creation, hubs of innovation, and catalysts for economic growth. Their operations often lead to a ripple effect in the economy: suppliers benefit from orders, employees spend their wages, and innovations lead to new industries. Moreover, businesses, through competition, drive the continuous improvement of products and services, ensuring that consumers get better choices and quality over time.

However, it's also essential to recognize that businesses have responsibilities. With their influence comes the duty to operate ethically, sustainably, and with consideration for the broader societal and environmental impact. The most successful and enduring businesses are often those that balance profit-making with purpose, ensuring that while they grow, they also uplift and contribute positively to the world around them.

In sum, a business is more than just a profit-seeking venture. It's a manifestation of human aspiration, a force of economic propulsion, and a cornerstone of modern society, intricately woven into the fabric of our daily lives and our collective future.

## 2.2 The Role of Supply and Demand

Supply and demand are foundational concepts in the world of economics and business, acting as the invisible hands that shape market dynamics. At its core, supply refers to the quantity of a product or service that producers are willing and able to offer for sale at different prices over a specific period. On the other hand, demand represents the quantity of a product or service that consumers are willing and able to purchase at various prices during a given timeframe.

The interplay between supply and demand determines the equilibrium price, or the price at which the quantity supplied equals the quantity demanded. When demand for a product rises, and all other factors remain constant, there's an upward pressure on its price. If producers can't keep up with this increased demand, shortages might occur, further driving up prices.

Conversely, if there's a decrease in demand for a product, its price tends to drop. If suppliers have excess stock due to decreased demand, they might reduce prices to clear out inventory.

Similarly, on the supply side, if there's an increase in the availability of a product but demand remains unchanged, there might be a surplus, leading to potential price reductions as businesses attempt to sell their excess stock. However, if there's a decrease in supply due to factors like production challenges or increased costs, and demand remains constant, prices might rise as consumers compete for the limited available stock.

It's also essential to understand that supply and demand are influenced by various external factors. For instance, technological advancements can increase supply by making production more efficient. In contrast, cultural trends or marketing campaigns can boost demand for specific products.

In the context of teaching children about business, understanding the role of supply and demand is crucial. It helps young entrepreneurs gauge market conditions, set appropriate prices, and anticipate changes. By mastering these concepts, they can make informed decisions, ensuring their business endeavors are both profitable and sustainable in the ever-evolving marketplace.

## 2.3 Introduction to Profit and Loss

In the world of business, two terms that are often at the forefront of any entrepreneur's mind are profit and loss. These concepts are fundamental to understanding the financial health and viability of a business venture. At its core, profit is the positive financial gain your business makes after all expenses have been deducted from the total revenue. It's the reward for the risks taken, the decisions made, and the strategies implemented.

On the other hand, a loss occurs when the total expenses exceed the revenue generated during a specific period, indicating that the business is spending more than it's earning.

The journey between generating a profit or incurring a loss is filled with various financial activities. For instance, when a child sets up a lemonade stand, they first invest in ingredients like lemons, sugar, and water. They might also spend on a poster board for advertising. The money they earn from selling each glass of lemonade is their revenue. Now, to determine if they've made a profit, they'd subtract the total amount spent on ingredients and other expenses from the total amount they earned from sales. If they earned more than they spent, they made a profit. If they earned less, they incurred a loss.

Understanding profit and loss is not just about numbers; it's about grasping the relationship between costs, pricing, and sales. It helps young entrepreneurs make informed decisions, such as whether to adjust the price of their product, cut down on certain expenses, or perhaps try a different marketing strategy to boost sales. Moreover, it instills a sense of responsibility and awareness about the importance of managing resources efficiently.

In the grand tapestry of business, profit and loss serve as critical indicators of success and areas of improvement. They provide insights into what's working and what's not, guiding entrepreneurs, even young ones, in their ongoing journey of learning, adapting, and growing. As children embark on their entrepreneurial adventures, a clear comprehension of these concepts will not only enhance their business acumen but also equip them with the financial literacy skills essential for life.

# Chapter: Cultivating an Entrepreneurial Mindset

Cultivating an entrepreneurial mindset in children is akin to planting a seed in fertile soil, ensuring that as they grow, they do so with a perspective that encourages innovation, resilience, and adaptability. This mindset is not just about starting a business; it's about approaching life's challenges with creativity and determination.

At the heart of an entrepreneurial mindset is the belief that problems are opportunities in disguise. When children are taught to view challenges not as insurmountable obstacles but as chances to innovate and learn, they begin to develop a proactive approach to life.

This perspective shift is crucial. Instead of waiting for opportunities to come their way, they seek them out, or even better, create them. This proactive stance is what differentiates entrepreneurs from others. They don't just adapt to change; they anticipate and leverage it.

Creativity and innovation are often hailed as the hallmarks of entrepreneurship. However, these qualities are not exclusive to the gifted few. Every child has a wellspring of creativity within them. What's essential is to nurture this creativity, allowing it to flourish without the fear of judgment or failure. Encouraging children to brainstorm, to question the status quo, and to dream without boundaries can unlock doors to imaginative solutions and groundbreaking ideas.

Yet, as vital as creativity is, it's equally important to instill a sense of resilience in young entrepreneurs. The journey of entrepreneurship is fraught with setbacks and failures. These are not just inevitable but are, in fact, invaluable. Each failure provides a lesson, and each setback paves the way for a comeback. By teaching children to view failures as stepping stones rather than stumbling blocks, we arm them with the tenacity to persevere.

This resilience, this ability to bounce back and push forward despite challenges, is often what separates successful entrepreneurs from those who give up.

Furthermore, an entrepreneurial mindset is also about adaptability. The world of business is dynamic, with markets, technologies, and consumer preferences constantly evolving. Children who learn to be flexible, who can pivot their strategies and adapt to changing circumstances, are better positioned to navigate the unpredictable waters of entrepreneurship. Adaptability also fosters a lifelong love for learning.

The thirst for knowledge, the curiosity to explore new horizons, and the humility to accept that there's always more to learn are traits that will serve young entrepreneurs well in their ventures and beyond.

Cultivating an entrepreneurial mindset in children is about more than just preparing them to start a business. It's about equipping them with a perspective that transforms challenges into opportunities, that values creativity and resilience, and that understands the importance of adaptability in an ever-changing world.

This mindset, once ingrained, becomes a powerful tool, not just in business but in every facet of life, empowering children to carve their paths, chase their dreams, and make a meaningful impact on the world around them.

## 3.1 The Value of Creativity and Innovation

Creativity, at its core, is the ability to conceive novel ideas, approaches, and solutions that may not conform to traditional methods. It's the spark that ignites the flame of possibility, allowing individuals to envision what might be rather than what is. This imaginative process is the foundation upon which all groundbreaking ventures are built, from the simplest lemonade stand to the most sophisticated tech startups.

Innovation, on the other hand, is the practical application of these creative ideas. It's the process of bringing a fresh concept to life, transforming imaginative visions into tangible realities. While creativity might be seen as the birth of a new idea, innovation is the nurturing and maturation of that idea into a product, service, or method that adds value to the market or society. Together, creativity and innovation form a dynamic duo that pushes the boundaries of what's possible, challenging the status quo and continuously reshaping industries.

In the context of teaching children about business, emphasizing the value of creativity and innovation is paramount. The young minds of today are the trailblazers of tomorrow, and by fostering their innate creative abilities, we equip them with the tools to not only adapt to the future but to shape it. Encouraging children to think outside the box, to question established norms, and to dream big can set them on a path of lifelong curiosity and ambition.

Moreover, in a world saturated with products, services, and brands, it's creativity and innovation that allow businesses to stand out from the crowd. They are the driving forces behind memorable marketing campaigns, revolutionary products, and customer loyalty. By understanding and appreciating the value of these elements, young entrepreneurs can position themselves ahead of the curve, ready to seize opportunities that others might overlook.

Creativity and innovation are more than just buzzwords in the business world; they are the lifeblood of progress and growth. By instilling their importance in the minds of young learners, we are not only preparing them for success in their entrepreneurial endeavors but also cultivating a mindset that will serve them well in all facets of life.

## 3.2 Overcoming Fear of Failure

In the journey of entrepreneurship, one of the most formidable obstacles that young minds often face is the fear of failure. This fear, deeply rooted in our psyche, can stem from various sources, be it societal expectations, peer pressure, or even our own self-imposed standards of success. Overcoming this fear is crucial, not just for business endeavors, but for personal growth and development as well.

To begin with, it's essential to understand that failure, contrary to popular belief, isn't the opposite of success; it's a part of it. Every renowned entrepreneur, from Steve Jobs to Oprah Winfrey, has faced setbacks and failures in their careers. What sets them apart is their ability to view these failures as learning opportunities, as stepping stones towards their ultimate goals. By reframing our perspective on failure, children can start to see it not as a dead-end, but as a detour or a lesson on the road to success.

Moreover, the fear of failure can often be linked to a fear of judgment. In our interconnected world, where achievements are often broadcasted and celebrated, it's easy for children to feel that they're constantly under the microscope, with every misstep being scrutinized. It's vital to instill in them the understanding that everyone, at some point, faces challenges and that it's okay to falter.

What's more important is the ability to pick oneself up, learn from the experience, and move forward with renewed determination.

Another strategy to combat this fear is to encourage children to set realistic and achievable goals. By breaking down a larger task into smaller, more manageable steps, the entire process becomes less daunting. Celebrating these small victories along the way can boost confidence and diminish the overwhelming fear that often accompanies large, seemingly insurmountable challenges.

Lastly, it's essential to foster a supportive environment where children feel safe to take risks and make mistakes. Whether it's parents, teachers, or mentors, having a strong support system can make a world of difference. When children know they have someone to turn to, someone who will guide them through their failures and celebrate their successes, they become more resilient and more willing to step out of their comfort zones.

Overcoming the fear of failure is a continuous process, one that requires a shift in perspective, a supportive environment, and the right tools and strategies. By addressing this fear head-on and equipping children with the means to face it, we're not just preparing them for the world of business but for life's many challenges and uncertainties.

## 3.3 Developing Resilience and Persistence

At the heart of resilience lies the ability to bounce back from setbacks, to face challenges head-on, and to adapt to changing circumstances without losing one's spirit or enthusiasm. It's about understanding that failure is not a reflection of one's worth but rather a stepping stone towards success. Every time a child encounters a hurdle in their business journey, it's an opportunity for them to learn, grow, and come back stronger.

Persistence, on the other hand, is the unwavering commitment to a goal, even in the face of repeated challenges or discouragements. It's the fuel that drives entrepreneurs to keep pushing forward, to keep refining their ideas, and to keep seeking solutions even when the path becomes tough. For children, developing persistence means cultivating a mindset where they see challenges as puzzles waiting to be solved rather than insurmountable obstacles. It's about fostering a belief that with enough effort and determination, any goal is achievable.

So, how do we instill these qualities in young entrepreneurs? It begins with setting the right expectations. Children should be made aware that the road to success is often paved with failures, mistakes, and rejections. But instead of perceiving these as negative outcomes, they should be viewed as learning experiences. When a child faces a setback, it's essential to encourage them to reflect on what went wrong, what they could do differently, and how they can improve in the future. This process of reflection and adaptation is at the core of resilience.

Furthermore, celebrating small victories along the way can significantly boost a child's persistence. Recognizing and applauding their efforts, even if they haven't reached their ultimate goal yet, can motivate them to keep going. It's also beneficial to expose children to stories of successful entrepreneurs who faced numerous challenges before achieving their dreams. Knowing that even the most successful individuals encounter hardships can provide children with the perspective and inspiration they need to persevere.

In essence, developing resilience and persistence in children is about equipping them with the right mindset and tools to navigate the unpredictable waters of entrepreneurship. It's about teaching them that setbacks are a natural part of the journey and that with determination, passion, and a willingness to learn, they can overcome any challenge and achieve their dreams.

# Chapter: Business Ideas for Kids

Children have already shown an incredible ability to innovate and create businesses that not only earn them pocket money but also teach invaluable life skills. When we think of business ideas suitable for kids, it's essential to consider ventures that are both age-appropriate and engaging, allowing them to harness their natural creativity and enthusiasm.

One of the most popular avenues young entrepreneurs explore is the world of handmade crafts. With platforms like Etsy and local craft fairs, children can turn their passion for art into a profitable venture. Whether they're making custom jewelry, designing unique t-shirts, or crafting homemade candles, there's a vast market for personalized items. This not only allows kids to express their creativity but also introduces them to the basics of product pricing, customer service, and marketing.

Another fantastic idea is pet care services. Many children love animals, and offering services like dog walking, pet sitting, or even basic grooming can be both fun and profitable. It's a great way for them to learn responsibility, time management, and interpersonal skills as they interact with both pets and their owners.

In the age of technology, many kids are more tech-savvy than adults. They can leverage this knowledge by offering basic tech support services to neighbors or.

family friends. This could range from setting up new devices, helping with software installations, or even giving lessons on how to use various platforms and apps. It's a brilliant way for them to capitalize on their tech skills while helping others.

Gardening and lawn care is another area where kids can shine. Whether it's mowing lawns, planting flowers, or setting up vegetable gardens, many homeowners appreciate the help. This type of work not only allows kids to earn money but also teaches them about nature, hard work, and the value of consistent effort.

Lastly, tutoring or teaching can be a rewarding experience for older kids. If they excel in a particular subject or have a hobby like playing a musical instrument, they can offer lessons to younger children. This not only reinforces their own knowledge but also helps them develop leadership and teaching skills.

The world of business offers a plethora of opportunities for kids to explore, learn, and grow. Whether they're tapping into their artistic side, leveraging their tech knowledge, or simply offering services in their community, there's no limit to what they can achieve with determination, creativity, and a bit of guidance.

## 4.1 Brainstorming Techniques

Brainstorming is a dynamic process that encourages individuals to come up with a myriad of ideas, often in a short span of time. It's a method that thrives on the principle that more ideas can lead to that one golden concept, especially when approached with an open mind. When teaching children about brainstorming, it's essential to emphasize the importance of free thinking and the belief that no idea is too outlandish.

One of the most popular techniques is the free-flow method, where children are encouraged to voice any idea that comes to their mind without any judgment or filtering. This spontaneous eruption of thoughts can often lead to unexpected and innovative solutions. It's like casting a wide net into the sea of creativity, hoping to catch a variety of ideas, some of which might be the seeds for a great business.

Another effective technique is the role-playing method. Children naturally have vivid imaginations, and by stepping into the shoes of different characters or personas, they can view problems and solutions from diverse perspectives. For instance, thinking from the viewpoint of an astronaut might lead to ideas related to space or technology, while imagining oneself as a farmer might bring forth concepts related to agriculture or sustainability.

Mind mapping is also a valuable tool in the brainstorming arsenal. By starting with a central idea and branching out with related concepts, children can visually map out their thoughts, making connections they might not have initially seen. This visual representation of ideas not only aids in clarity but also fosters a deeper understanding of how different concepts interrelate.

The challenge and solution method can be particularly effective. Here, children are presented with a specific problem or challenge, and they brainstorm ways to solve it. By focusing their creative energies on addressing a particular issue, they often come up with targeted and practical business ideas.

Incorporating these techniques into brainstorming sessions can be both fun and educational for children. It nurtures their creativity, boosts their problem-solving skills, and lays the foundation for innovative thinking, which is crucial in the world of entrepreneurship.

## 4.2 Evaluating Business Ideas

Evaluating business ideas is a crucial step in the entrepreneurial journey, especially for young minds eager to dive into their first venture. At the heart of this evaluation lies the question: "Is this idea viable and does it have the potential to succeed?" To answer this, one must consider several intertwined factors.

Firstly, there's the matter of passion and interest. An idea might be commercially viable, but if the child isn't genuinely excited about it, the energy to push through challenges might wane.

It's essential to strike a balance between what's profitable and what genuinely interests the young entrepreneur. This passion often becomes the driving force behind perseverance, creativity, and the willingness to learn and adapt.

Next, we must consider the target market. Who are the potential customers? Understanding the audience is pivotal. It's not just about identifying them but also diving deep into their needs, preferences, and pain points. A successful business idea often addresses a particular need or solves a specific problem for its target audience. For children, this might mean identifying gaps in the market that cater to their peers or even recognizing needs in their local community.

Cost is another significant factor. While children might not have substantial financial resources, it's essential to understand the basic costs associated with starting and running the business. Will they need initial capital for materials or advertising? Are there ongoing costs to consider? It's a delicate balance of ensuring the idea is financially feasible without compromising on the quality of the product or service.

Furthermore, the uniqueness of the idea plays a role. In today's saturated market, what sets one business apart is often its unique selling proposition (USP). For a child's business idea, this doesn't necessarily mean inventing something entirely new but could be about offering a fresh perspective or a unique twist on an existing product or service.

Lastly, feedback is invaluable. Before diving headfirst into an idea, it's beneficial to seek opinions from trusted individuals, be it parents, teachers, or peers. They can offer a different perspective, highlight potential challenges, or even suggest ways to enhance the idea further.

It's all about ensuring that the idea not only resonates with the child's interests but also has the potential to thrive in the market. Through careful consideration and a touch of creativity, young entrepreneurs can pave the way for a successful and fulfilling business journey.

## 4.3 Case Studies: Successful Kid Entrepreneurs

In the world of entrepreneurship, age is but a number. The stories of young entrepreneurs breaking barriers and achieving success are both inspiring and instructive. Let's delve into a few remarkable tales of kids who turned their dreams into reality.

One of the most notable stories is that of Emma,

a 10-year-old who had a passion for baking. Living in a small town in Vermont, she noticed that many of her neighbors were looking for organic, gluten-free baked goods, but had to travel miles to the nearest city to find them. Sensing an opportunity, Emma began experimenting with recipes in her kitchen. She soon developed a line of delicious, gluten-free cookies and muffins. Word of mouth spread quickly, and before she knew it, she was receiving bulk orders from local cafes and stores. Emma's story is a testament to the power of identifying a niche market and catering to its needs with passion and dedication.

Consider the story of Lucas, a 13-year-old from Oregon with a deep concern for the environment. After learning about the harmful effects of plastic waste in school, Lucas was determined to make a difference. He started collecting discarded plastic bottles from his neighborhood and, using a simple home-based process, transformed them into colorful, eco-friendly coasters. His products quickly gained traction at local craft fairs and online marketplaces. Lucas's venture not only became profitable but also raised awareness about recycling and sustainable living.

Another inspiring tale is that of Aisha, an 11-year-old from Atlanta. Aisha loved reading but noticed that there were very few children's books that featured characters of diverse backgrounds. Recognizing this gap, she began writing her own stories, highlighting the adventures of young heroes from different cultures. With the support of her parents, she self-published her first book, which was met with enthusiastic reviews from teachers, parents, and kids alike. Aisha's initiative not only catered to a market need but also championed the cause of representation and inclusivity in children's literature.

Then there's the story of twins Mia and Ava, 12-year-olds from Chicago. The duo was passionate about fashion and often designed outfits for their dolls. Realizing that many kids their age shared their interest, they started a YouTube channel offering DIY fashion tutorials for dolls. Their engaging content, combined with their infectious enthusiasm, quickly garnered a massive following. Capitalizing on their online success, they launched a line of doll clothing and accessories, turning their hobby into a thriving business.

Lastly, think of Leo, a 14-year-old from Texas. Leo's family owned a farm, and he grew up understanding the value of fresh produce. Recognizing that many urban residents lacked access to fresh, organic vegetables, Leo started a subscription-based service delivering farm-fresh produce to doorsteps. His commitment to quality and customer service turned his venture into a favorite among health-conscious families in his city.

Raj, a 12-year-old tech whiz from San Francisco. Raj was always fascinated by the world of technology, often taking apart gadgets to understand their inner workings. One day, while trying to help his grandmother set up her new smartphone, he realized that many older adults struggled with modern technology. This sparked an idea: a user-friendly app that would guide seniors through the basics of using smartphones and tablets. With the help of online coding tutorials and a few mentors, Raj developed his app, which became a hit in senior communities across the state. His success underscores the importance of solving real-world problems and the limitless potential of technology.

Sofia, a 9-year-old from New Mexico enjoyed creating intricate bead jewelry, a skill she learned from her grandmother. Recognizing the uniqueness of her designs, she decided to set up a stall at a local farmer's market. The response was overwhelming. People were not only drawn to her beautiful creations but also to the story behind them. Capitalizing on this, Sofia started hosting workshops, teaching other kids the art of bead jewelry making. Her venture not only became a source of income but also a platform to promote creativity and cultural heritage among her peers.

Each of these young entrepreneurs had a unique journey, but common threads run through their stories. They all identified a need, pursued their passions, and were not afraid to take risks. Their successes serve as a beacon of inspiration for other kids and even adults, reminding us that with determination, innovation, and a bit of courage, anything is possible.

These stories further emphasize the incredible capabilities of young minds. Whether driven by passion, a desire to solve problems, or simply the thrill of creating something new, these young entrepreneurs have shown that age is no barrier to success in the world of business. Their journeys inspire and challenge us to think outside the box and to never underestimate the power of youthful determination.

# Chapter: Creating a Business Plan

Creating a business plan is akin to charting a course for an adventurous voyage. It's the blueprint that guides entrepreneurs through the tumultuous waters of business, ensuring they have a clear vision of their destination and the means to get there. At its core, a business plan is a reflection of an entrepreneur's dreams translated into actionable steps, grounded in research and analysis.

For children embarking on their entrepreneurial journey, the process of crafting a business plan can be both enlightening and empowering. It's not just about jotting down ideas on paper; it's about diving deep into the heart of what they want to achieve, understanding the market they're entering, and visualizing the path to success.

The first step in creating a business plan is understanding its purpose. While many might think it's solely for attracting investors or securing loans, a business plan serves a more fundamental role. It acts as a compass, ensuring that young entrepreneurs remain focused on their goals, making informed decisions based on facts and figures rather than mere whims or assumptions.

A well-structured business plan begins with an executive summary. This section provides a snapshot of the business, encapsulating its essence in a concise manner. It's the elevator pitch, the first impression, and it sets the tone for what's to follow.

Following the executive summary, a detailed description of the business is essential. This is where the child entrepreneur paints a vivid picture of their business idea, describing the products or services they intend to offer, their unique selling proposition, and the problem they aim to solve in the market.

Market analysis is the backbone of any robust business plan. It's where young entrepreneurs delve into the intricacies of their target market, understanding customer demographics, preferences, and behaviors. By analyzing competitors and identifying market trends, they can carve out a niche for themselves, ensuring their business idea isn't just a fleeting thought but has a solid foundation in reality.

Financial projections, though perhaps daunting for some, are crucial. They provide a glimpse into the potential profitability of the business. By estimating revenues, costs, and profits, young entrepreneurs can gauge the viability of their business idea. It's a reality check, ensuring they're not venturing into a financial abyss but are on a path that has the potential for monetary success.

Business plan should outline the operational strategy.

This encompasses everything from sourcing materials to production processes, distribution channels, and customer service protocols. It's the nuts and bolts of how the business will function on a day-to-day basis.

Creating a business plan is a rite of passage for every entrepreneur, young or old. It's a testament to their commitment, passion, and vision. For children, the process is not just about launching a business; it's a learning experience, teaching them the importance of research, planning, and strategic thinking. With a well-crafted business plan in hand, they're not just dreamers; they're doers, ready to turn their entrepreneurial dreams into reality.

## 5.1 The Purpose of a Business Plan

A business plan serves as a roadmap for an entrepreneurial journey, guiding both young and seasoned entrepreneurs through the multifaceted world of business. It's not just a document but a reflection of an entrepreneur's vision, ambition, and commitment to turning an idea into a tangible reality. By articulating the mission, vision, and values of the business, it provides a clear direction and sets the tone for the entire venture. Beyond this foundational role, a business plan is instrumental in detailing the strategies that will be employed to achieve specific objectives, from market penetration to revenue generation.

Furthermore, it delves into the intricacies of the target market, offering insights into customer behaviors, preferences, and potential challenges in capturing market share. This understanding is pivotal, as it shapes the marketing, operational, and financial strategies that will be employed. Speaking of finances, a business plan meticulously outlines the financial health and projections of the business, ensuring that there's a clear understanding of the capital required, the revenue streams, and the potential profitability. This financial blueprint not only keeps the business on track but also instills confidence in potential investors, lenders, and other stakeholders, showcasing the viability and potential return on investment.

A business plan acts as a tool for reflection and adaptation. The business environment is dynamic, with challenges and opportunities emerging at every turn. By regularly revisiting and updating the business plan, entrepreneurs can assess their progress, recalibrate their strategies, and make informed decisions that align with the changing landscape. In essence, a business plan is more than just a document; it's the lifeblood of a business, ensuring clarity, direction, and a strategic approach to the entrepreneurial journey.

## 5.2 Key Components of a Business Plan

One of the primary components of a business plan is the executive summary, which provides a snapshot of the entire plan, capturing the essence of the business and its potential in a concise manner. This is often followed by a detailed description of the business itself, including its structure, the products or services it offers, and the unique value proposition it brings to the market.

Understanding the market is crucial, so a comprehensive market analysis is another vital component. This section delves into the target audience, their needs and preferences, and the competitive landscape. It identifies potential opportunities and threats and helps in positioning the business effectively in the market. The operational plan then outlines the day-to-day activities of the business, detailing how it will deliver its products or services, the logistics involved, and the resources required, including manpower, equipment, and technology.

Financial projections, another key component, provide a forecast of the business's financial performance. This section includes projected income statements, balance sheets, and cash flow statements, offering insights into the expected profitability and financial health of the business. It's essential for attracting investors and lenders, as it showcases the potential return on investment and the business's ability to manage its finances effectively.

The marketing and sales strategy is where the business plan outlines how the company plans to attract and retain customers. This involves a mix of promotional strategies, pricing models, sales tactics, and distribution channels that the business channels that the business will employ to reach its target audience and drive sales. Lastly, a business plan should also address potential risks and challenges. By identifying potential pitfalls and having contingency plans in place, the business demonstrates foresight and preparedness, which can instill confidence in stakeholders and potential investors.

In essence, a business plan is a cohesive document that intertwines various elements, from the vision and mission of the business to its operational and financial strategies, all aimed at ensuring the business's success and sustainability in the market.

## 5.3 Simplifying the Process for Kids

Teaching children about the intricacies of business planning doesn't mean overwhelming them with complex jargon or intricate details. Instead, it's about breaking down the process into digestible chunks and presenting it in a manner that resonates with their level of understanding. When simplifying the business planning process for kids, it's essential to start with the core idea of what they want to achieve with their business. This can be as simple as helping them articulate their primary goal, whether it's selling handmade crafts to friends and family or setting up a lemonade stand in their neighborhood.

Once the core idea is established, guide them to think about the basic resources they'll need. This doesn't have to be a detailed inventory list but rather a general understanding of what's necessary to get started. For instance, for a lemonade stand, they'd need lemons, sugar, water, and perhaps a stand or table. By focusing on these tangible elements, children can begin to visualize the steps they need to take.

Next, introduce the concept of customers. Who are they? Why would they be interested in the product or service? Encourage children to think about what makes their offering unique and how they can communicate that to potential customers. This can be a fun exercise, as kids can tap into their creativity, thinking about colorful signs for their lemonade stand or special promotions like a "buy one, get one free" offer.

Budgeting is another crucial aspect, but it doesn't have to be complicated. At its core, it's about understanding how much things cost and how much money they might make. Use simple math to help them figure out potential profits, subtracting the cost of materials from the price they plan to charge.Lastly, remind them that every business will face challenges, but these are opportunities to learn and grow. Whether it's rain on the day of their lemonade stand or running out of materials for their crafts, these experiences teach resilience and problem-solving.In essence, simplifying the business planning process for kids is about making it relatable, tangible, and engaging. It's not about dumbing down the content but rather presenting it in a way that aligns with their curiosity and enthusiasm for learning.

# Chapter: Understanding Finances

Understanding finances is a cornerstone of any successful business venture, and it's no different when teaching children about entrepreneurship. At the heart of every business lies the fundamental concept of money management, which encompasses the inflow and outflow of funds, ensuring that the business remains viable and profitable.

When we delve into the world of finances, we're not just talking about counting coins or bills. We're discussing the intricate dance of balancing income with expenses, of understanding where every penny goes, and of ensuring that there's more coming in than going out. For a child, this might seem like a daunting task, but with the right guidance, it can become an enlightening and empowering experience.

One of the first things to grasp is the concept of revenue. This is the total amount of money brought into the business, primarily from selling goods or services. It's the lifeblood of any enterprise. However, revenue alone doesn't determine success. From this total, businesses must deduct their expenses, which can range from the cost of raw materials to marketing efforts, to arrive at a profit. Profit is what remains after all expenses have been accounted for, and it's a clear indicator of the business's health.

Pricing strategies play a pivotal role in determining both revenue and profit. Setting the right price for a product or service is a delicate balance. Price too high, and potential customers might be deterred; price too low, and the business might not cover its costs or make a profit. It's essential to understand the cost of producing a product or delivering a service and then factor in a margin that ensures profitability while still offering value to the customer.

Equally important is the art of tracking income and expenses. Without a clear record of financial transactions, it's easy for money to slip through the cracks, leading to potential losses or missed opportunities for growth. Even in the simplest of businesses run by children, maintaining a ledger or a basic record of money coming in and going out can provide invaluable insights. It helps identify patterns, understand seasonal fluctuations, and make informed decisions about future investments or expansions.

Budgeting is another crucial aspect of financial understanding. It's the act of forecasting future income and expenses, allowing for better planning and preparation. By setting a budget, young entrepreneurs can set clear goals, prioritize spending, and ensure they have enough funds for both current operations and future growth.

In the world of business, unexpected expenses are inevitable. Therefore, it's wise to set aside a portion of profits as a safety net or emergency fund. This practice not only teaches children the importance of saving but also prepares them for unforeseen challenges, ensuring their business can weather any financial storm.

While the world of finances might seem complex, it's built on a few fundamental principles. By mastering these basics, young entrepreneurs can set themselves up for a lifetime of successful business ventures, ensuring they not only understand the value of money but also how to make it work for them.

## 6.1 Basics of Money Management

Money management is a foundational skill that not only plays a pivotal role in the world of business but also in our personal lives. At its core, money management revolves around understanding how money flows in and out, and making informed decisions to ensure financial stability and growth. When children embark on their entrepreneurial journey, it's essential for them to grasp the importance of being financially literate.

Starting with the concept of income, it's the money that a business earns from selling products or services. Every business, no matter how small, will have some form of income, and it's crucial to keep a meticulous record of it. This income serves as the lifeblood of the business, fueling its operations and potential expansions. However, just as there's money coming in, there are also expenses. Expenses encompass everything the business spends money on, from raw materials to marketing campaigns. It's vital to track every penny spent to understand where the money is going and to identify areas for potential savings.

Budgeting is another cornerstone of money management. It involves planning how to spend the income in a way that covers all expenses while also setting aside a portion for savings or future investments. A well-structured budget acts as a roadmap, guiding young entrepreneurs in making strategic financial decisions. It helps them anticipate potential financial challenges and prepare for them.

Moreover, the concept of saving cannot be stressed enough. Even a small business should aim to save a portion of its earnings. These savings can act as a safety net during lean times or be used for future investments to grow the business. Furthermore, understanding the value of savings early on instills a sense of financial responsibility and foresight.

Lastly, while it might seem advanced for children, the idea of investment is worth introducing. Investments are essentially avenues where money can be placed to grow over time, whether it's reinvesting back into the business, buying assets, or even exploring simple financial instruments suitable for their age. By understanding the basics of investment, children can learn the power of making their money work for them.

Money management is a blend of tracking, planning, saving, and investing. By mastering these basics, young entrepreneurs set themselves up for a future where they can make informed financial decisions, ensuring the longevity and success of their business endeavors.

## 6.2 Pricing Strategies

Pricing is one of the most critical aspects of a business, especially for young entrepreneurs who are just starting out. It's a delicate balance between ensuring profitability and offering a price that's attractive to potential customers. When determining the right pricing strategy, it's essential to consider both the cost of producing the product or service and the perceived value it offers to the customer.

Starting with the cost-based approach, this method involves calculating the total cost of producing a product or delivering a service and then adding a desired profit margin. For instance, if a child entrepreneur is making handcrafted bracelets and the materials cost $5, and they want to make a profit of $3 per bracelet, they would price it at $8. This approach ensures that all costs are covered and a profit is made with each sale.

However, cost isn't the only factor to consider. The perceived value plays a significant role in pricing. Sometimes, the value a product or service offers to a customer can be much higher than its production cost. For example, a unique piece of art or a personalized service might have a higher perceived value, allowing for a higher price point. It's essential to gauge what customers are willing to pay based on the uniqueness, quality, and emotional connection they have with the product or service.

Competitor-based pricing is another strategy to consider. By researching what competitors or similar businesses are charging, young entrepreneurs can position their prices competitively. If their product has added features or benefits, they might price slightly higher, or if they're looking to quickly penetrate a market, they might opt for a slightly lower price.

Another consideration is psychological pricing. This strategy taps into the way customers perceive prices. For instance, pricing a product at $9.99 instead of $10 can make it seem more affordable, even though the difference is just a penny. This method can be particularly effective in retail settings where small differences can influence purchasing decisions.

Lastly, it's crucial to remember that pricing isn't static. As the business grows, costs change, or the market evolves, revisiting and adjusting the pricing strategy becomes necessary. Regularly reviewing prices and being open to feedback can help young entrepreneurs stay competitive and ensure their business remains profitable in the long run.

Determining the right pricing strategy requires a blend of

understanding costs, gauging perceived value, researching competitors, and tapping into psychological pricing techniques. With careful consideration and regular reviews, young entrepreneurs can set prices that support both their business's growth and their customers' needs

## 6.3 Tracking Income and Expenses

In the world of business, especially when teaching children the fundamentals, understanding the flow of money is paramount. Tracking income and expenses is not just about recording numbers; it's about painting a clear picture of the financial health of a venture. When children embark on their entrepreneurial journey, they quickly realize that money coming in, often termed as 'income' or 'revenue', is a positive affirmation of their efforts. It's the tangible reward for a product sold or a service rendered. However, it's only one side of the coin.

On the flip side, there are expenses, which are the costs incurred to generate that income. These can range from the simple, like buying materials to create handmade crafts, to the more complex, such as marketing costs or fees for online platforms. It's essential to understand that every business will have expenses, and they are a natural part of the entrepreneurial process.

By diligently tracking both income and expenses, young entrepreneurs can gain insights into their profit margins, which is the difference between their total income and total expenses.

This difference determines whether a business is making money or running at a loss. Moreover, understanding where the money is coming from and where it's going can empower children to make informed decisions. For instance, if they notice a particular expense is consistently high, they might brainstorm ways to reduce it or find alternatives. Conversely, if a specific product or service is generating significant income, they might decide to focus more on that area.

Furthermore, maintaining a clear record of financial transactions provides a historical perspective. Over time, children can analyze trends, predict future cash flows, and make strategic decisions based on past data. For example, if they observe that their business income spikes during the holiday season, they can prepare in advance for the next one, ensuring they have enough stock or capacity to meet the increased demand.

Tracking income and expenses is like telling the story of a business through numbers. It offers a snapshot of the present, a record of the past, and a predictor of the future. By instilling this practice early on, we're not just teaching children to be better entrepreneurs; we're equipping them with financial literacy skills that will benefit them throughout their lives, regardless of the path they choose.

# Chapter: Marketing and Promotion

Marketing is a comprehensive process that encompasses the understanding of one's target audience, their needs, preferences, and the channels they frequent. It's about crafting a narrative, a story that resonates with potential customers, making them feel connected to the product or service being offered.

Promotion, on the other hand, is the act of pushing that narrative forward, ensuring it reaches the right ears and eyes. In today's digital age, promotion often intertwines with platforms like social media, online advertising, and influencer partnerships. But it's essential to remember that the essence of promotion goes beyond mere visibility. It's about engagement, creating a dialogue with the audience, and fostering a community that believes in the brand's values and vision.

One might wonder why these two elements are so crucial. The answer lies in the vast sea of competition. With countless businesses vying for a slice of the market pie, standing out becomes not just a challenge but a necessity. And that's where effective marketing and promotion come into play. By understanding the unique selling proposition (USP) of a business and positioning it effectively in the market, one can carve out a niche, a space where their product or service is not just seen but sought after.

However, the journey doesn't end there. The world of marketing and promotion is ever-evolving, with trends shifting and consumer behaviors changing. It's a dance of adaptation, where businesses must stay on their toes, continually reinventing their strategies to stay relevant and appealing. This dynamic nature is what makes marketing and promotion so exhilarating. Every campaign, every promotional event, is an opportunity to learn, adapt, and grow, ensuring that the brand remains etched in the minds of consumers, not as a fleeting memory, but as a lasting impression.

## 7.1 Branding Basics

Branding is the art and science of creating a distinct identity for a business or product, making it stand out in the minds of consumers. At its core, branding is about storytelling, weaving a narrative that resonates with your target audience, and evokes emotions that drive loyalty and trust. When we think of iconic brands, we often recall not just a logo or a catchy slogan, but a feeling, an experience, or a memory associated with that brand.

In the world of business, especially for young entrepreneurs, understanding the essence of branding can be the difference between blending in and standing out. It's not just about having a memorable logo or a vibrant color scheme; it's about the promise you make to your customers and how consistently you deliver on that promise. Every interaction, whether it's through a product, service, advertisement, or even a social media post, should reflect the brand's values and mission.

For children starting a business, it's essential to recognize that branding begins with clarity. Before diving into design elements, they should be clear about what their business stands for, who it aims to serve, and what makes it unique. This foundational understanding will guide all subsequent branding decisions, ensuring coherence and authenticity.

Moreover, branding is an ongoing process. As the business grows and evolves, so too will its brand. Feedback from customers, market trends, and personal growth as an entrepreneur can all influence the direction a brand takes. It's crucial to remain flexible and open to change, but also to stay true to the core values and promises that define the brand.

Branding is a journey of discovery and expression. It's about finding the heart and soul of a business and communicating it in a way that captivates and connects with the audience. For young entrepreneurs, mastering the basics of branding can pave the way for lasting success, creating a legacy that goes beyond products and profits, touching lives and making a difference.

## 7.2 Social Media for Kids

For children, navigating the vast world of social media can be both an exciting journey and a challenging endeavor.

It's a space where they can express themselves, connect with friends, and even discover new educational content. However, it's essential to approach social media with a sense of caution and awareness, especially for younger users.

Firstly, it's crucial to recognize that not all social media platforms are suitable for children. While some platforms cater specifically to younger audiences with age-appropriate content and safety measures, others might expose them to content beyond their maturity level. Parents and guardians should take an active role in understanding the platforms their children are interested in and ensuring they align with their age and understanding.

Safety is paramount. Children should be educated about the importance of not sharing personal information, such as their full name, address, school, or phone number. They should also be made aware of the potential risks of interacting with strangers online. It's not just about the information they share, but also about understanding the digital footprint they leave behind. Every post, like, and share contributes to their online persona, which can have long-term implications.

Moreover, while social media can be a source of inspiration and creativity, it can also lead to issues like cyberbullying or feelings of inadequacy when comparing oneself to others. It's essential to foster open communication with children, allowing them to discuss their experiences, feelings, and concerns about what they encounter online. By creating a supportive environment, children can learn to use social media responsibly, understanding its benefits and potential pitfalls.

Lastly, balance is key. While social media can offer numerous learning and social opportunities, it's essential to ensure that children also spend time offline, engaging in physical activities, reading, and other non-digital pursuits. This balance ensures a holistic development, where children can harness the advantages of the digital world while also remaining grounded in the tangible world around them.

Social media for kids can be a double-edged sword. With the right guidance, education, and oversight, it can be a tool for growth, learning, and connection. However, without proper understanding and boundaries, it can also present challenges. It's up to adults to guide the younger generation through this digital landscape, ensuring they reap the benefits while staying safe and informed.

## 7.3 Traditional Marketing Techniques

It might seem that traditional marketing techniques have taken a backseat, but they remain as potent and effective as ever, especially when targeting local audiences or specific demographics that might not be as digitally connected. One of the cornerstones of traditional marketing is print advertising. Newspapers, magazines, and brochures have been trusted channels for decades, offering businesses the opportunity to reach audiences in a tactile and tangible way. These mediums allow for creative expression, from compelling visuals to persuasive copy, capturing the attention of readers in a manner that's often more immersive than digital ads.

Beyond print, radio advertising stands as a testament to the power of voice and sound. A catchy jingle or a compelling story told over the airwaves can resonate with listeners, creating a memorable brand impression. Radio's strength lies in its ability to reach people during moments when other forms of media might not, such as during commutes or household chores.

Television advertising, with its combination of visuals, sound, and motion, offers a multisensory experience that can be both entertaining and informative. The power of a well-crafted TV commercial lies in its ability to evoke emotions, be it laughter, nostalgia, or excitement, making the brand or product memorable to viewers.

Outdoor advertising, including billboards and posters, provides visibility in high-traffic areas, ensuring that a brand's message is seen by a vast number of people. These larger-than-life advertisements can become local landmarks, especially when placed strategically at busy intersections or popular city spots.
Direct mail, often perceived as old-fashioned, has a

personal touch that's hard to replicate digitally. Receiving a physical piece of mail, be it a postcard, a catalog, or a special offer, can make the recipient feel valued and singled out, especially when the content is tailored to their preferences or past interactions with the brand.

Face-to-face marketing, through trade shows, seminars, and networking events, allows businesses to build direct relationships with potential customers. There's an inherent trust that's established when people meet in person, making these interactions invaluable for building brand loyalty and understanding customer needs.

Incorporating these traditional marketing techniques into a broader strategy, alongside digital methods, ensures a holistic approach that reaches diverse audiences and maximizes brand visibility.

# Chapter: Operations and Logistics

Operations and logistics form the backbone of any successful business venture, especially when we consider the intricate dance of coordinating resources, time, and effort to bring a product or service to the market.

At its core, operations encompass the day-to-day activities that keep a business running smoothly. This includes everything from sourcing raw materials, managing inventory, to ensuring that products are produced and delivered in a timely and efficient manner. It's the art and science of ensuring that the cogs of the business machine mesh seamlessly.

Logistics, on the other hand, delves deeper into the movement and transportation aspects. It's about getting the right product, in the right quantity, to the right place, at the right time. In the age of globalization, logistics has become even more crucial. Imagine a toy manufacturer based in Europe wanting to sell products in Asia. The journey of the toy, from the factory floor to the hands of a child in Tokyo or Mumbai, is a testament to the marvel of modern logistics.

Both operations and logistics require meticulous planning and foresight. Without a well-oiled operational process, businesses can face bottlenecks, where a hiccup in one part of the production line can cause delays and inefficiencies downstream. Similarly, without effective logistics, products might not reach their intended market, or they might arrive damaged or late, leading to dissatisfied customers and potential financial losses.

Moreover, in today's fast-paced world, consumers have come to expect quick and reliable services. The rise of e-commerce giants has set a precedent where customers anticipate next-day or even same-day deliveries. This puts immense pressure on businesses, both big and small, to optimize their operational and logistical frameworks. It's no longer just about getting a product out; it's about doing it faster, better, and more efficiently than before.

Incorporating technology has been a game-changer in this realm. Advanced software can now predict inventory needs, optimize routes for delivery, and even automate certain operational processes. The integration of artificial intelligence and machine learning means that these systems can continuously learn and improve, adapting to changes in real-time.

Operations and logistics are more than just business buzzwords. They represent the intricate choreography of activities and processes that bring a business idea to life. In a world where efficiency and speed are paramount, mastering these two areas is not just beneficial—it's essential for any business aiming for long-term success and sustainability.

## 8.1 Sourcing Materials and Inventory Management

Especially when it comes to young entrepreneurs, understanding the intricacies of sourcing materials and managing inventory is paramount. Sourcing materials is the process of finding, selecting, and procuring the necessary components or products required to create a final offering. This can range from raw materials for crafting to finished products for resale. The key is to identify suppliers who offer quality materials at competitive prices, ensuring that the end product is both high-quality and cost-effective. Building strong relationships with suppliers can lead to better negotiation terms, ensuring timely deliveries and even potential discounts.

On the other hand, inventory management is the art and science of maintaining an optimal level of stock. It's a delicate balance: holding too much inventory can tie up capital and increase storage costs, while too little can lead to stockouts, missed sales, and disappointed customers. Effective inventory management requires a keen understanding of demand patterns, which can be influenced by seasonality, market trends, or promotional activities. It's also crucial to have a system in place, whether manual or digital, to track inventory levels, sales, and reorder points. This ensures that stock is replenished in a timely manner, minimizing holding costs and maximizing sales opportunities.

As businesses grow, the challenges of sourcing and inventory management can become more complex. It might involve dealing with multiple suppliers, managing backorders, or even navigating international shipping and customs for imported goods. Therefore, it's essential to continuously educate oneself, possibly seeking expert advice or utilizing specialized software solutions to streamline these processes. In the end, mastering both sourcing and inventory management can significantly impact a business's efficiency, profitability, and overall success.

## 8.2 Setting Up a Workspace

Setting up an effective workspace for a child entrepreneur is a delicate balance between functionality and inspiration. It's not just about having a desk and a chair; it's about creating an environment that fosters creativity, concentration, and a sense of ownership. The space should resonate with the child's personality, allowing them to feel both comfortable and motivated.

Location is paramount. While it might be tempting to tuck the workspace in a quiet corner of the house, it's essential to consider the child's need for both focus and supervision. A spot that's too isolated might lead to distractions, while a place that's too central might be too bustling for concentration. Ideally, the workspace should be in a location where the child can have some privacy but is still within the purview of an adult, ensuring safety and guidance when necessary.

Lighting plays a crucial role in any workspace. Natural light can boost mood and productivity, so if possible, position the workspace near a window. However, ensure that there's also adequate artificial lighting for those cloudy days or evening work sessions. Adjustable lamps can be particularly useful, allowing the child to direct light where it's most needed.

Ergonomics shouldn't be overlooked, even for young entrepreneurs. Investing in a chair that offers good support and a desk at the right height can make a significant difference in comfort. Remember, children are still growing, so it's essential to ensure that their posture isn't compromised.

Storage is another key consideration. While we want to encourage children to think big, their workspace might be limited in size. Utilizing vertical space with shelves, pegboards, or magnetic boards can be a great way to keep essential tools and materials organized without cluttering the desk surface.

Personalization can turn a generic workspace into a haven of inspiration. Allow the child to decorate their space with items that inspire them, be it artwork, motivational quotes, or mementos from their entrepreneurial journey. This not only makes the space feel like their own but also serves as a daily reminder of their goals and aspirations.

Lastly, technology and tools should be tailored to the child's business needs. While a computer might be essential for some, others might benefit more from crafting tools or a drawing board. It's essential to equip the workspace with tools that align with the child's business endeavors, ensuring they have everything they need at their fingertips.

## 8.3 Time Management and Productivity

Especially when starting out, time is an invaluable asset. It's often said that time is money, and for young entrepreneurs, this couldn't be truer. Managing time effectively is the cornerstone of productivity, and productivity is the engine that propels a business forward. When children embark on their entrepreneurial journey, they are not just juggling their business tasks but also their schoolwork, extracurricular activities, and personal time. This makes mastering time management even more crucial.

One of the first steps in effective time management is understanding the distinction between urgent tasks and important tasks. Urgent tasks demand immediate attention, but they might not necessarily contribute to the long-term goals or vision of the business. On the other hand, important tasks are those that align with the business's objectives and often have long-term benefits, even if they don't seem pressing in the immediate moment. By prioritizing important tasks over merely urgent ones, young entrepreneurs can ensure that they are constantly moving in the direction of their goals. Another key aspect of time management is the art of delegation. Even in small ventures, there might be tasks that can be handed off to others, freeing up the entrepreneur to focus on more critical aspects of the business. This is a valuable lesson for children to learn early on: they don't have to do everything themselves. By seeking help when needed, they can optimize their time and resources.

Moreover, integrating tools and technology can be a game-changer. In today's digital age, there are numerous apps and platforms designed to assist with scheduling, task tracking, and reminders. While it's essential not to become overly reliant on technology, using it strategically can streamline operations and boost productivity.

It's also worth noting that breaks are not the enemy of productivity; in fact, they can be its ally. Periodic breaks can refresh the mind, reduce stress, and improve overall efficiency. Especially for young minds, it's essential to balance work with relaxation to maintain enthusiasm and creativity.

Lastly, setting clear and realistic goals can act as a compass, guiding young entrepreneurs in allocating their time effectively. When they know what they're working towards, it becomes easier to prioritize tasks and manage their time in a way that brings them closer to their objectives.

Time management and productivity go hand in hand. For

young entrepreneurs, mastering these skills early on can set the foundation for a successful and fulfilling business journey.

# Chapter: Legal and Ethical Considerations

Starting with the legal side of things, every business, regardless of its size or the age of its founder, is subject to certain regulations. These regulations are in place to ensure fair competition, protect consumers, and maintain the integrity of the market. For instance, even a simple lemonade stand run by a child might require a permit in certain jurisdictions. While this might seem excessive, it's a testament to the importance of adhering to local laws. Ignorance of these laws is rarely accepted as an excuse, and penalties can range from fines to the shutting down of the business. Therefore, it's crucial for young entrepreneurs, with the guidance of their guardians, to familiarize themselves with local business regulations and ensure they are in compliance.

Beyond the tangible laws and regulations, there's the matter of ethics. Ethics refers to the moral principles that guide our actions. In business, this translates to practices that might be legal but are considered morally questionable. For example, while it might be legal to sell a product at a high markup, is it ethical to do so if the product is of low quality or if it's being marketed in a deceptive manner? Young entrepreneurs must grapple with these questions early on. They must decide what kind of businesspeople they want to be: those who prioritize profits above all else or those who believe in fair and honest dealings.

Moreover, ethical considerations extend beyond transactions. They encompass how a business interacts with its community, environment, and even competitors. Is the business sourcing its materials in a sustainable manner? Is it giving back to the community in some way? Is it treating its competitors with respect and not engaging in slander or other negative tactics? These are all questions that young business owners must consider.

In many ways, teaching children about legal and ethical considerations is about more than just business. It's about instilling in them a sense of responsibility, integrity, and respect for the world around them. It's about teaching them that success is not just measured in dollars and cents but in the impact one has on the world and the legacy one leaves behind.

While the legal and ethical landscape of business can be complex, it offers young entrepreneurs a valuable opportunity to learn and grow. By navigating this landscape with care and consideration, they can build businesses that are not only profitable but also a force for good in the world.

## 9.1 Understanding Business Licenses and Permits

Starting a business, even for children, often involves navigating the world of licenses and permits. These are official documents issued by governmental bodies that grant permission to individuals or entities to conduct specific business activities within a particular jurisdiction.

They serve as a means to ensure that businesses operate within the confines of the law, maintain certain standards, and protect the interests of the public.

At the heart of understanding business licenses and permits is recognizing their primary purpose: to regulate industries, protect consumers, and ensure public safety. For instance, a restaurant would need health permits to ensure it meets hygiene standards, while a business that plays music might need a license to avoid copyright infringement.

For young entrepreneurs, the type of business they wish to start will largely dictate the licenses and permits required. For example, if a child wants to start a lemonade stand, they might need a temporary vendor's license, especially if they plan to set up in public spaces. On the other hand, if they're thinking of selling handmade crafts online, they might need to look into e-commerce regulations and permits.

It's also essential to understand that licenses and permits come from various levels of government. Some might be issued at the local city or town level, while others come from the state or even federal level. The geographical location of the business, therefore, plays a significant role in determining which licenses are necessary. For instance, a child operating a business in one city might face different licensing requirements than if they were in a neighboring town.

Moreover, the process of obtaining these licenses and

permits can vary. Some might involve simple online registration, while others could require inspections, tests, or even attending courses. Fees are often associated with these processes, and they can range from nominal amounts to more substantial sums, depending on the nature of the license or permit.

While the world of business licenses and permits might seem daunting, especially for young entrepreneurs, it's a crucial aspect of ensuring that a business operates legally and ethically. It's always advisable for children, with the guidance of their parents or mentors, to research and understand the specific requirements for their business idea in their particular location. This not only ensures compliance but also instills a sense of responsibility and understanding of the broader business landscape.

## 9.2 Safety and Privacy Concerns

Where businesses, even those started by children, often have an online presence, the importance of safety and privacy cannot be overstated. As young entrepreneurs venture into the world of business, they are exposed to a myriad of potential risks, both online and offline. Online platforms, while offering immense opportunities for marketing and sales, also present challenges in terms of data protection and cyber threats. Children, in particular, can be vulnerable targets for malicious actors who might exploit their limited experience or knowledge.

One of the primary concerns is the sharing of personal information. Young business owners might inadvertently disclose sensitive details, such as home addresses, school names, or even daily routines, which can pose direct threats to their physical safety.

Moreover, the collection of customer data, if not handled with care, can lead to breaches of privacy, potentially damaging the reputation of the business and leading to legal ramifications.

Furthermore, the use of digital tools and platforms necessitates an understanding of cybersecurity. Without adequate protective measures, businesses can fall prey to cyberattacks, ranging from phishing scams to more sophisticated hacking attempts. For children, who might not yet be fully aware of the intricacies of online security, this poses a significant risk.

Additionally, there's the matter of online interactions. Engaging with customers or followers on social media or through email can expose young entrepreneurs to inappropriate content or potentially harmful individuals. It's crucial for them to recognize the signs of suspicious behavior and know when and how to disengage.

While the entrepreneurial journey for children offers invaluable learning experiences and opportunities for growth, it's imperative to navigate it with a keen awareness of safety and privacy concerns. By fostering a culture of caution and educating young business owners about potential risks, we can ensure that their ventures are not only successful but also secure.

## 9.3 Ethical Business Practices

Ethical business practices refer to the adherence to moral principles and standards that guide the behavior of individuals and organizations in their business interactions. These practices are not just about obeying laws and regulations, but also about recognizing and acting upon the broader responsibilities businesses have to society, their stakeholders, and the environment.

At the heart of ethical business practices is the commitment to fairness. This means treating customers, employees, suppliers, and competitors with respect and honesty. For instance, businesses should provide products and services that are of promised quality and value, and they should not engage in deceptive marketing or advertising. When it comes to employees, ethical businesses ensure safe working conditions, fair wages, and opportunities for growth and development. They avoid discriminatory practices and respect the rights and dignity of all individuals.

Furthermore, ethical businesses are transparent in their operations. They are open about their financial dealings, their challenges, and their successes. This transparency builds trust with stakeholders, from investors to customers, and ensures that the business is held accountable for its actions. In today's digital age, where information is easily accessible, businesses that hide facts or manipulate information can quickly lose their credibility and trustworthiness.

Another cornerstone of ethical business practices is the commitment to sustainability. This means recognizing the impact of business operations on the environment and taking proactive steps to minimize negative effects. Ethical businesses consider the long-term consequences of their actions and strive to create a balance between profitability and environmental responsibility.

Moreover, ethical businesses also consider their role in the community. They recognize that their success is intertwined with the well-being of the society in which they operate. As a result, many engage in philanthropic activities, support local initiatives, or establish programs that give back to the community in meaningful ways.

As consumers become more conscious of the ethical practices of companies they engage with, businesses that uphold high ethical standards are more likely to thrive and succeed in the competitive marketplace.

# Chapter: Mentorship and Support

For a child stepping into the vast world of business, having a mentor can be likened to having a compass in an uncharted territory. It provides direction, clarity, and, most importantly, confidence.

Imagine a young mind, brimming with ideas and enthusiasm, but uncertain about the path ahead. This is where a mentor, with their wealth of experience and knowledge, steps in. They don't just offer advice on business strategies or financial decisions; they provide insights into the very fabric of the entrepreneurial world. They share stories of their successes, their failures, and the lessons they've learned along the way. These narratives are invaluable, offering both cautionary tales and inspirational anecdotes that can shape a child's entrepreneurial journey.

But mentorship isn't just about the transfer of knowledge. It's about building a relationship based on trust, respect, and mutual growth. A mentor doesn't merely instruct; they listen. They understand the unique challenges faced by their young protégé and offer tailored guidance. They celebrate the successes, no matter how small, and provide a shoulder to lean on during the inevitable setbacks.

Parents and guardians, too, play a pivotal role in this ecosystem of support. While they might not always have the business acumen or experience, their emotional support, encouragement, and belief in their child's vision can be the driving force behind many young entrepreneurs. Their role is to create a safe environment where a child feels free to dream, to experiment, and even to fail. Because in failure, often lie the most profound lessons.

Furthermore, the community around a young entrepreneur can offer a network of support. Joining groups or clubs focused on kid entrepreneurship can be a game-changer. It's not just about networking in the traditional sense; it's about finding peers who share similar dreams and challenges. Such groups can become a space for collaboration, where ideas are exchanged, partnerships are formed, and lifelong friendships are forged.

While the technicalities of starting a business, like finances, marketing, and operations, are undeniably crucial, the human element of mentorship and support is the backbone of a successful entrepreneurial journey. It's the safety net that allows a child to take risks, the guiding light in moments of doubt, and the cheerleading squad celebrating every milestone. In the world of business, as in life, it's not just about the destination but the people who accompany you on the journey.

## 10.1 The Role of Parents and Guardians

In the entrepreneurial journey of a child, parents and guardians play an indispensable role that extends beyond mere supervision. Their involvement is a blend of guidance, encouragement, and real-world insight, acting as the foundational support system for young business enthusiasts. From the earliest stages of recognizing a child's interest in entrepreneurship, it is the parents and guardians who often become the first sounding board for their ideas. They provide a safe space for children to express their visions, dreams, and even apprehensions.

As children navigate the complexities of starting a business, parents and guardians serve as both mentors and cheerleaders. Their life experiences, combined with their intimate understanding of their child's strengths and weaknesses, position them uniquely to offer tailored advice. They can share stories of their own successes and failures, imparting lessons about resilience, perseverance, and the value of hard work. Moreover, their encouragement can be the driving force that propels a child forward during challenging times, reminding them of their capabilities and the importance of persistence.

Financial aspects of starting a business, especially for children, can be daunting. Here, parents and guardians play a crucial role in imparting financial literacy. They can help children understand the basics of budgeting, saving, and investing, ensuring that the young entrepreneurs are not just business-savvy but also financially astute.

Furthermore, the emotional well-being of a child entrepreneur is paramount. The world of business, with its highs and lows, can be emotionally taxing. Parents and guardians, with their nurturing instincts, can ensure that children maintain a healthy balance between their business pursuits and other aspects of their lives. They can teach them the importance of taking breaks, seeking help when needed, and understanding that it's okay to make mistakes.

While the entrepreneurial spirit may be innate in many children, it is the unwavering support, guidance, and love from parents and guardians that truly allows it to flourish. Their role is not just about providing resources or capital but about fostering a mindset that equips children to face the business world with confidence, knowledge, and a heart full of passion.

## 10.2 Finding a Business Mentor

Finding a business mentor is a pivotal step in a young entrepreneur's journey, acting as a bridge between the raw enthusiasm of a novice and the seasoned experience of a veteran. A mentor provides not just knowledge, but also offers insights, perspectives, and lessons that textbooks and courses might miss. The process of finding the right mentor requires a blend of proactive outreach, genuine curiosity, and a bit of patience.

Begin by identifying what you hope to gain from the

mentorship. Are you seeking guidance on a specific business challenge, or are you looking for general advice on entrepreneurship? Knowing your objectives will help you target potential mentors who align with your needs. Remember, a mentor doesn't necessarily have to be in the same industry as you; sometimes, the most valuable insights come from those who have faced different challenges and can offer a fresh perspective.

Networking is a powerful tool in the search for a mentor. Attend local business events, workshops, and seminars. Engage in conversations, ask questions, and listen actively. Often, these events are frequented by experienced professionals who might be open to mentoring or can introduce you to potential mentors. Don't be shy about expressing your interest in finding a mentor; many seasoned professionals remember their early days and are eager to give back.

Online platforms, such as LinkedIn, can also be instrumental. By joining groups related to your business interests, you can engage with potential mentors, share your journey, and ask for advice. When reaching out, be genuine and specific about why you believe they would be a great mentor for you. Personalize your message and show that you've done your homework about their background and achievements.

While finding a mentor is essential, it's equally crucial to ensure that the relationship is mutually beneficial. A mentorship is a two-way street. Be respectful of your mentor's time, come prepared with questions, and be open to feedback, even if it's tough to hear. Over time, as trust and rapport build, you'll find that the mentor-mentee relationship can evolve into a lasting professional bond that benefits both parties.

The journey to find a business mentor might require effort and persistence, the rewards in terms of knowledge, growth, and networking are immeasurable. Embrace the process, be genuine in your approach, and remember that every interaction is a learning opportunity.

## 10.3 Joining Kid Entrepreneur Groups

There's a unique and vibrant subset dedicated to nurturing the budding business minds of children: Kid Entrepreneur Groups. These groups serve as a nexus where young innovators come together, not just to share their business ideas, but to foster a sense of community, collaboration, and mutual growth. Joining such a group can be a transformative experience for a young entrepreneur.

Imagine a space where a child, brimming with ideas, meets peers who are equally passionate. This environment is not just about competition but about learning from one another. In these groups, children often find that their innovative ideas are met with enthusiasm, constructive feedback, and sometimes, even collaboration offers. It's a place where a child's lemonade stand concept can evolve into a community project or where handmade crafts can find their way to local markets with the collective effort of the group.

Moreover, these groups often host workshops, seminars, and guest sessions with seasoned entrepreneurs who offer insights, share their journeys, and provide mentorship. Such interactions can be invaluable, giving children a real-world perspective on the challenges and rewards of running a business. It's one thing to learn about entrepreneurship from books or in a classroom, but it's entirely another to hear firsthand accounts from those who've walked the path.

Beyond the tangible benefits of knowledge and collaboration, there's an emotional and psychological boost that children gain from these groups. Entrepreneurship can be a lonely journey, filled with uncertainties. Being part of a group provides a safety net, a place to share successes, navigate failures, and simply know that they're not alone in their endeavors. It instills confidence, teaches them the importance of networking, and reinforces the idea that while entrepreneurship is about individual vision, it's also about collective growth and support.

Joining a Kid Entrepreneur Group is not just about business; it's about belonging, growing, and realizing that even in the world of business, there's strength in numbers and unity.

# Chapter: Scaling and Growth

The concepts of scaling and growth are often intertwined, yet they possess distinct nuances that are vital for young entrepreneurs to grasp. As children embark on their entrepreneurial journeys, understanding these principles can be the difference between a fleeting venture and a sustainable, long-term business.

Scaling, at its core, refers to the ability of a business to handle increased demands without compromising performance or efficiency. It's not just about growing in size or revenue, but about growing smartly. Imagine a lemonade stand that becomes so popular that the line of customers stretches around the block. If the young entrepreneur behind it simply tries to serve more and more customers without refining their process, they might end up overwhelmed, with long wait times and frustrated customers. However, if they find ways to serve multiple customers at once, perhaps by setting up multiple serving stations or pre-pouring batches of lemonade, they've effectively scaled their operations.

Growth, on the other hand, is a broader concept. It encompasses the expansion of a business in various dimensions, be it in terms of revenue, customer base, product offerings, or geographical presence. Growth can be the result of effective scaling, but it can also come from diversifying products, entering new markets, or leveraging marketing strategies to reach a wider audience.

For young entrepreneurs, the journey of scaling and growth begins with self-awareness. Recognizing the current capacities of their business and identifying the bottlenecks is the first step. For instance, if a child's handmade jewelry business is booming, but they can only make a limited number of pieces each day, they might consider collaborating with friends, streamlining the production process, or even exploring third-party manufacturers as they grow.

Yet, with growth comes challenges. It's essential for young business minds to remain adaptable. The strategies and approaches that worked in the initial stages of the business might not be as effective as the business grows. This adaptability might mean adopting new technologies, learning about different market segments, or even rebranding to appeal to a broader audience.

Moreover, as businesses scale and grow, the importance of maintaining quality cannot be overstated. It's easy to get caught up in the excitement of expansion, but compromising on the quality that initially attracted customers can be detrimental. Young entrepreneurs must remember that their reputation is invaluable. Consistency in delivering value, even as they evolve, will ensure that their growth is sustainable.

Scaling and growth are exciting phases in the entrepreneurial journey. They offer opportunities for increased profits, wider recognition, and the satisfaction of seeing one's vision expand beyond initial boundaries. However, they also come with their set of challenges. By approaching these phases with a combination of enthusiasm, adaptability, and a commitment to quality, young entrepreneurs can navigate the complexities of scaling and growth, setting their businesses up for long-term success.

## 11.1 When and How to Expand

Expanding a business is a thrilling yet challenging phase in an entrepreneur's journey, even more so when the entrepreneur is a young individual. Recognizing the right moment to expand is crucial. Often, the signs are a consistent increase in demand, a steady revenue stream that exceeds expectations, and feedback from customers suggesting the need for more products, services, or locations. Additionally, when the current operations run smoothly and there's a sense that the business has outgrown its initial setup, it might be time to consider expansion.

However, knowing when to expand is just one piece of the puzzle. The 'how' is equally, if not more, important. Expansion doesn't always mean opening a new location or branching out into a different product line. Sometimes, it's about deepening the offerings within the current niche or improving the quality and efficiency of existing products or services. For young entrepreneurs, it's essential to approach expansion with a mix of enthusiasm and caution.

Before making any moves, it's wise to conduct thorough market research. Understand where the demand is coming from, what competitors are doing, and where there might be gaps in the market that your business can fill. This research will provide a clearer picture of the opportunities and challenges that lie ahead.

Financing is another critical aspect of expansion. While it might be tempting to reinvest all the profits, young entrepreneurs should consider diverse funding options. These might include loans, grants, partnerships, or even crowdfunding, depending on the nature and scale of the expansion. It's also essential to have a clear financial plan that outlines the expected costs and projected revenue from the expansion.

Furthermore, expanding a business often means expanding the team. Hiring the right people, those who share the business's vision and values, can make a significant difference in the expansion's success. Training and integrating new team members effectively ensures that the business maintains its quality and reputation as it grows.

Staying true to the brand, listening to loyal customers, and being adaptable in the face of new challenges will serve young entrepreneurs well as they navigate the complexities of growth.

## 11.2 Diversifying Product or Service Offerings

When we talk about diversifying product or service offerings, we're referring to the process of adding new products or services to a business's portfolio, or modifying existing ones, to appeal to a broader customer base or to tap into new markets. This strategy can be particularly beneficial for young entrepreneurs as it not only provides multiple streams of revenue but also acts as a safety net against unforeseen market downturns.

Imagine a child starting a business selling handmade bracelets. While the initial product might gain traction, there's a limit to how many bracelets a single customer might buy. By diversifying and introducing related products such as necklaces, earrings, or even DIY jewelry-making kits, the young entrepreneur can cater to a wider audience, ensuring that the business remains relevant and continues to grow. Moreover, diversification can also be a response to seasonal changes. For instance, a kid running a lemonade stand in the summer might switch to selling hot cocoa in the winter.

However, diversification isn't just about adding more to the mix; it's about strategic expansion. It's essential to conduct market research to understand what the customers truly want and to identify gaps in the market. For instance, if our young bracelet maker notices a trend in sustainable or upcycled jewelry, they might consider introducing a line of products made from recycled materials. This not only taps into a new market segment but also positions the business as environmentally conscious.

Furthermore, diversifying offerings also means being adaptable. The business landscape, even for kid entrepreneurs, is ever-evolving. Trends change, customer preferences shift, and new technologies emerge. By being open to diversification, young business minds can learn the importance of adaptability, innovation, and forward-thinking. They'll understand that while it's essential to have a core product or service that defines the brand, it's equally crucial to be flexible and responsive to the changing needs of the market.

Diversifying product or service offerings is a proactive approach to business growth. It encourages innovation, reduces dependency on a single revenue stream, and prepares young entrepreneurs for the unpredictable yet exciting journey of running a business.

## 11.3 Planning for the Future

The ability to look ahead and envision the trajectory of one's enterprise is not just a skill, but a necessity. When teaching children about starting a business, it's essential to emphasize the importance of future planning. This doesn't mean merely thinking about the next product ilaunch or sales event, but truly contemplating the long-term vision and mission of their business endeavor.

Planning for the future involves a blend of imagina
tion, foresight, and practicality. Children, with their innate creativity, often have a plethora of ideas. The challenge lies in channeling this creativity into a structured vision for their business. Encourage them to dream big, but also to ground these dreams in reality. For instance, if a child's business revolves around crafting handmade toys, they might envision expanding into an entire line of children's products or even opening their own toy store one day. While these are ambitious goals, they are not unattainable with the right planning.

Furthermore, future planning also encompasses the ability to anticipate challenges and obstacles. The business landscape is fraught with unpredictability, from market fluctuations to evolving consumer preferences. By teaching children to be adaptable and to always have a contingency plan, they'll be better equipped to navigate these uncertainties. This adaptability is not about fearing change, but embracing it as an opportunity for growth and innovation.

Another crucial aspect of planning for the future is financial foresight. While immediate profits might be tempting, it's vital for young entrepreneurs to understand the value of reinvestment. Allocating resources for future projects, expansion, or even unforeseen expenses ensures the longevity and sustainability of their business. This also means understanding the difference between short-term gains and long-term benefits. For example, investing in a marketing campaign now might mean fewer profits in the immediate term, but it could significantly boost brand awareness and customer loyalty in the long run.

Lastly, as children plan for the future of their business, it's also a good time to remind them of their personal growth journey. The skills, experiences, and lessons they gain from running a business will be invaluable in all facets of their lives. Whether they continue with entrepreneurship or venture into different fields, the discipline, resilience, and problem-solving abilities they develop will undoubtedly serve them well.

Planning for the future is about more than just business strategy; it's about cultivating a mindset that is forward-thinking, proactive, and ever-curious about the possibilities that lie ahead.

# Conclusion from the Author

## Celebrating Successes and Learning from Failures

Celebrating successes isn't just about acknowledging the milestones achieved but also about reinforcing the positive behaviors, strategies, and decisions that led to those victories. Every time a child entrepreneur achieves a goal, whether it's making their first sale, receiving positive feedback, or even just completing a business plan, it's a testament to their hard work, dedication, and the application of the lessons they've learned. Celebrating these moments boosts their confidence, motivates them to push forward, and instills a sense of pride in their accomplishments.

However, just as the sun is complemented by the rain, successes in business are often accompanied by failures. And while failures might seem discouraging at first glance, they are, in fact, invaluable learning opportunities. Instead of viewing failures as setbacks, it's crucial to perceive them as stepping stones towards greater understanding and growth. Every mistake made, every challenge faced, and every obstacle encountered provides insights into areas of improvement, offering lessons that textbooks and lectures often can't.

When a young entrepreneur faces a failure, it's an opportunity to analyze what went wrong, to understand the underlying reasons, and to adapt strategies for the future. It teaches resilience, problem-solving, and the art of perseverance. Moreover, failures help children develop emotional intelligence, as they learn to manage disappointment, frustration, and the ability to bounce back with renewed vigor.

In the grand tapestry of entrepreneurship, successes are the bright, vibrant threads that stand out, capturing attention and admiration. In contrast, failures are the underlying stitches, often unseen but holding everything together, providing strength and structure. Together, they weave a story of growth, learning, and evolution. By celebrating successes and embracing failures, young entrepreneurs not only equip themselves with the tools and mindset needed for the business world but also for the broader challenges of life.

## The Lifelong Benefits of Early Entrepreneurship

In the journey of life, the seeds we plant during our formative years often bear the most significant fruits. Introducing children to the world of entrepreneurship is not just about teaching them how to start a business or make money. It's about instilling a mindset that can transform their approach to challenges, opportunities, and personal growth. Early entrepreneurship education fosters a spirit of self-reliance, teaching children that they have the power to shape their destinies. They learn that failures are not setbacks but stepping stones, each one offering invaluable lessons that pave the way for future successes.

fMoreover, the world of entrepreneurship nurtures creativity and innovation. Children are naturally imaginative, and when we channel this innate ability towards problem-solving in a business context, we empower them to see the world not just as it is, but as it could be. They begin to view challenges as puzzles waiting to be solved, and this perspective can be applied in every facet of their lives, from personal relationships to academic pursuits and beyond.

Furthermore, early exposure to business teaches children about the value of hard work, dedication, and perseverance. They come to understand that while instant gratification is tempting, the most rewarding achievements are often those that require time, effort, and patience. This understanding of delayed gratification can influence their decisions and priorities in various aspects of life, from financial management to personal development.

Additionally, entrepreneurship fosters interpersonal skills. As children navigate the world of business, they interact with a diverse range of individuals, from customers to suppliers, mentors, and peers. These interactions teach them about communication, negotiation, and empathy, skills that are invaluable in both professional and personal spheres.

In essence, the benefits of early entrepreneurship extend far beyond the realm of business. It shapes character, molds perspective, and equips children with a toolkit of skills and attitudes that will serve them in every endeavor they undertake. As they grow into adults, these early lessons in entrepreneurship will stand them in good stead, helping them navigate the complexities of the modern world with confidence, resilience, and a proactive spirit. So, as we close this chapter, let's remember that by fostering entrepreneurial spirits in our young ones, we're not just teaching them to start businesses; we're setting them on a path to a fulfilling, empowered life.

www.ingramcontent.com/pod-product-compliance
Lightning Source LLC
Chambersburg PA
CBHW072332290526
45794CB00002B/835